Rosalyn Thompson This Is Your Life Part 1

Reading Comprehension Workbook

Master Edition

(Episode 1)

The Move

---

1. Why were the Thompsons moving?
They were moving because Mr. Thompson got a promotion at his job.

2. Name three reasons Rosalyn didn't want to move.
She didn't want to move because she didn't want to live in a new neighborhood, she didn't want to go to a new school and she didn't want to make new friends.

3. What was Rosalyn going to miss the most about Caymen Point? She would miss her best friend Monica the most.

4. Why did Rosalyn finally have to leave the house after they moved? She finally left the house because her mom wanted her to go to the store and get some cornmeal.

5. Explain what you would miss most if you had to move to another city. (Answers will vary)

__REFLECTION__

Describe your overall thoughts of this episode.

Answers will vary.

(Episode 2)

The Meeting

---

1. How did Rosalyn react when the girl questioned her at the store? Rosalyn was unfriendly and acted as if it was a bother to answer.

2. When Rosalyn came home from the store who knocked on the door for her? One of the girls from the store followed her home and knocked on the door for her.

3. Who did her dad think was at the door at first? Her dad thought it was her grandmother at first.

4. What did Rosalyn's dad tell her she would eventually have to do? Her dad told her she would eventually have to make friends in Sherwood.

REFLECTION

Describe your overall thoughts of this episode.

Answers will vary.

(Episode 3)

The Visit

---

1. What gifts did Rosalyn's grandmother bring for the family? Her grandmother brought her a stuffed animal with money. She brought her mom cutlery for cooking and she brought her dad a new wallet.

2. Why did her grandmother get Mr. Thompson his gift? She brought him a new wallet because she said his old one was raggedy and worn out.

3. Rosalyn's grandmother asked her to go somewhere with her. Where was it? Her grandmother asked her to go to church.

4. How did her parents feel about her going with her grandmother? Her parents were excited about her going to church with her grandmother.

5. Why do you think they felt this way? They felt this way because they wanted her to get out of the house.

<u>REFLECTION</u>

Describe your overall thoughts of this episode.

Answers will vary.

(Episode 4)

The Surprise

---

1. Who did Rosalyn and her grandmother run into in the lobby of the church? They ran into Sister Banks in the lobby.

2. What was the surprise at church? Rosalyn was surprised to see the other girl from the store at church.

3. How did Rosalyn feel about all the questions Zoey was asking her? Rosalyn felt like Zoey was being nosy and prying.

4. Where did she think hanging with Zoey could get her? She thought hanging with Zoey could get her into trouble with her parents.

REFLECTION

Describe your overall thoughts of this episode.

Answers will vary.

(Episode 5)

The Fall

---

1. How did Rosalyn's parents feel about her going to the skating rink with Sharice and Zoey? Her parents were excited that she was getting out of the house and making new friends.

2. How did she feel when the two girls left her alone at the table? Rosalyn felt alone and uncomfortable when she was at the table by herself.

3. Describe Rosalyn's emotions after she fell. After Rosalyn fell she felt embarrassed and was ready to go home.

4. What did Rosalyn decide to do when Sharice and Zoey came back to check on her? Rosalyn decided to go back skating when the girls came back for her.

5. Why do you think she did this? What would you have done? (Answers will vary)

REFLECTION

Describe your overall thoughts of this episode.

Answers will vary.

(Episode 6)

Just Business

---

1. Why did Sharice and Zoey keep calling Rosalyn? They kept calling Rosalyn because they wanted to know what she wanted them to tell Kevin Johnson.

2. Where were Rosalyn and her mother going? Rosalyn and her mother were going to a catering show downtown.

3. What person from Mrs. Thompson's past did they see at the event? They saw Dana at the catering event.

4. Explain this person's relationship to Mrs. Thompson. Mrs. Thompson and Dana use to be business partners.

5. Describe Rosalyn's emotions after running into Kevin and his dad. Rosalyn was nervous and had butterflies in her stomach.

REFLECTION

Describe your overall thoughts of this episode.

Answers will vary.

(Episode 7)

The Sleepover

---

1. **Explain how Sharice and Zoey's feelings differed toward having a boyfriend.** Sharice felt like it wasn't important to have a boyfriend and Zoey felt like she needed to have one at all times.

2. **Were Rosalyn's feelings toward having a boyfriend more like Sharice's or Zoey's?** Rosalyn's feelings were more like Sharice's. She felt it wasn't that important to have a boyfriend.

3. **What activity had Rosalyn been involved in for years before moving to Sherwood?** Rosalyn had been involved in dance before she moved to Sherwood.

4. **What did the girls decide they were going to do for the up and coming school year?** The girls decided they were going to try out for the school dance team.

REFLECTION

Describe your overall thoughts of this episode.

Answers will vary.

(Episode 8)

The Talk

---

1. **Why did Rosalyn's mom want to talk to her?** Her mom wanted to talk to her because she had been hearing Rosalyn's phone conversations about boys.

2. **What advice did she give Rosalyn?** Her advice to Rosalyn was to never let anyone get in the way of what she wanted and for her to stay focused.

3. **How did talking to Monica make Rosalyn feel?** Talking to Monica made Rosalyn feel like everything was going to be okay.

4. **What did Rosalyn and Monica promise to do before they got off the phone?** The two girls promised to have Monica come visit over the holidays.

5. **Has talking to a friend ever made you feel better? Why or why not?** (Answers will vary)

REFLECTION

Describe your overall thoughts of this episode.

Answers will vary.

(Episode 9)

The Turning Point

---

1. The evening of the turning point where did Mrs. Thompson go? That evening Mrs. Thompson went to a catering event.

2. What was the turning point? The turning point was when Mrs. Thompson died in a car accident.

3. Explain Rosalyn's emotions after the turning point. After her mom died, Rosalyn went into a deep depression. She was heartbroken and extremely sad. She wondered why she had to go through the rest of her life without her mom.

4. What did Rosalyn's Grandmother do to make her feel better? Her grandmother decided to take her shopping and to get a makeover.

5. Who did they see at the mall? They saw Sharice and Zoey at the mall.

REFLECTION

Describe your overall thoughts of this episode.

Answers will vary.

(Episode 10)

Tryouts

1. At the beginning of the episode Rosalyn wasn't sure if they should still try out for the dance team. Why was she feeling this way? Rosalyn wasn't sure if they should try out for the dance team because they didn't have much time to make up their routine and perfect it.

2. Once they arrived at tryouts, Sharice and Zoey weren't sure if they wanted to try out. What made Sharice change her mind and want to try out again? Sharice changed her mind about trying out when the "goonie bunch" walked by and rolled their eyes.

3. Why did Rosalyn sit and stare after the names of the new dance team members were called? She sat and stared because she was thinking about how happy her mom would be that they all made the team.

4. What did the girls decide to do on behalf of Mrs. Thompson? The girls decided they would dedicate their dance season to Mrs. Thompson.

REFLECTION

Describe your overall thoughts of this episode.

Answers will vary.

Describe the similarities and differences between Rosalyn, Sharice and Zoey in the Venn diagram below.

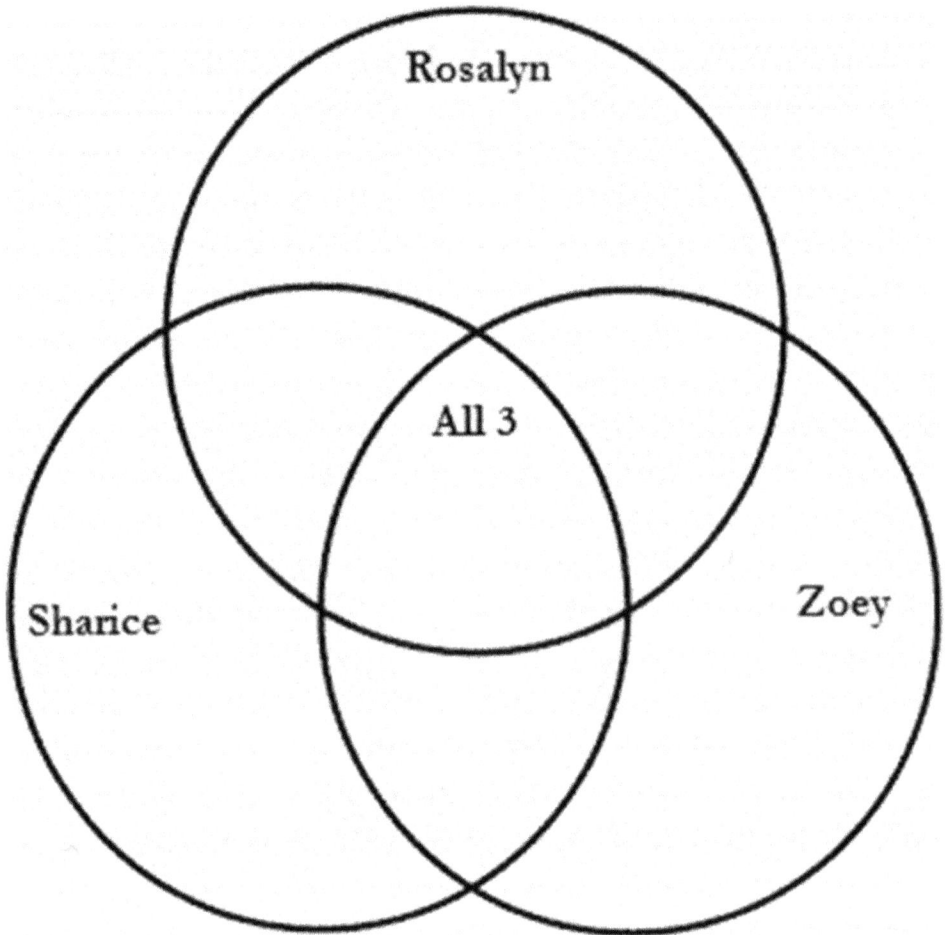

Rosalyn

All 3

Sharice

Zoey